Ray Kroc
Famous Restaurant Owner

Marilyn Mascola

illustrated by Luciano Lazzarino

Rourke Enterprises  Vero Beach, Florida

Manufactured in the United States of America

Library of Congress Cataloging-in-Publication Data

Mascola, Marilyn, 1949-
    Ray Kroc : famous restaurant owner / by Marilyn
Mascola.
        p.   cm. —(Reaching your goal)
    Summary: A biography of the businessman whose
purchase of a small restaurant in the 1950s resulted in the
international chain of McDonald's restaurants. Includes
information on setting goals.
    1. Kroc, Ray, 1902-   —Juvenile literature. 2.
Restaurateurs—United States—Biography—Juvenile
literature.
3. McDonald's Corporation—Juvenile literature. [1. Kroc,
Ray, 1902-   . 2. Restaurateurs. 3. McDonald's
Corporation.] I. Title. II. Series: Reaching your goal.
TX910.5.K76M37 1989
388.7′61647′9509—dc19
[B]   88-26341
[92]   CIP
ISBN 0-86592-433-3   AC

"Raymond! It's time to come in and practice," called Mrs. Kroc.

Ray liked to play the piano, but he also liked playing baseball with his friends. Baseball was Ray's favorite sport. He was one of the best players at his grade school in Oak Park, Illinois. He was also a big Chicago Cubs fan.

Ray's mother taught Ray to play the piano. She also gave piano lessons to bring in extra money. Ray and his brother and sister were all expected to help out with the housework.

Ray didn't mind. He liked thing to be neat and clean. He helped make the beds, sweep the floor, and clean the rugs.

Ray liked keeping busy. He was always thinking of new ways to do things. These were usually ways to make money. His mother thought he was daydreaming and called him Danny Dreamer.

At a very young age, Ray started earning money. One summer he had a lemonade stand. Another summer, when he was still in grade school, he worked at a grocery store. Later, he worked at his uncle's drugstore. There was no doubt about it — he loved to work!

Ray saved almost every penny he earned. He dreamed of owning his own business some day.

Ray was still in high school when he started his first business. With two friends, he opened a music store. They sold sheet music and instruments. Ray played the music on the piano to interest customers in buying it. Everyone enjoyed hearing Ray play, but few people bought music.

As a child, Ray didn't enjoy reading. In high school, the only subject he liked was debate. In debate, you must try to convince the audience that your side is right. Ray was good at convincing people.

After tenth grade, Ray quit school. World War 1 had started, and he wanted to fight in the war. He was only 15, but he lied about his age. He became an ambulance driver for the Red Cross.

After the war, Ray returned to Chicago. During the day he sold ribbons, and at night he played jazz piano. One summer he was playing in a band and he met Ethel Fleming. Three years later, they got married.

Ray got a steady job selling paper cups for the Lily Company. At that time, paper cups were new. Ray had to talk fast to convince his customers to buy them.

Drugstores, restaurants, and other businesses bought paper cups from Ray. In the winter, business slowed down. They didn't use as many paper cups.

One winter, Ray decided to try his luck in Florida. He had read that people were buying land there. He decided to move there for five months and sell it to them!

Soon, though, people stopped buying land. Ray lost his job but found another one playing the piano in a fancy nightclub. But Ethel was homesick for Chicago. They decided to move back early.

Ray put Ethel and their daughter, Marilyn, on the train to Chicago. He drove their Ford Model T home. It was open at the top and the sides. As Ray drove north, the temperature dropped. Ray wasn't wearing a warm coat or gloves. By the time he reached Chicago, he was nearly frozen.

Ray went back to his old job at the Lily Company. He worked hard and was soon promoted to manager. Then he met Earl Prince. Mr. Prince had invented a wonderful machine, the Multimixer. It mixed six milk shakes at one time. Other machines could only mix one.

12

Ray quit his job with the paper cup company. He began a new business selling Multimixers. Dairy Queen, Tastee Freeze, and A&W all bought Multimixers from Ray. By this time, the Multimixer had been changed. It only mixed five shakes at a time.

In 1954, Ray went to visit a restaurant in California. He had heard that they owned eight Multimixers. What kind of restaurant needs so many Multimixers? Ray wondered. This he had to see for himself! He flew to San Bernadino, California. There he visited Maurice and Dick McDonald's hamburger stand.

Ray arrived at McDonald's at 10 A.M. He watched the workers arrive wearing crisp, white uniforms and white paper hats. They moved sacks of potatoes, beef, buns, and other supplies into the kitchen. At 11 o'clock, they were ready to open. A line had formed in front of the restaurant, and the parking lot was full.

McDonald's only sold hamburgers, french fries, milk shakes, and soft drinks. Most other restaurants offered a wider choice. But McDonald's prices were cheaper than other places, and their food was good.

15

Ray talked to the customers. They all praised McDonald's. Then he talked to Maurice and Dick McDonald. They gave him a tour and told him how McDonald's worked. Making the hamburgers was divided into easy steps. Every time, the work was done the same way. That way, every hamburger turned out exactly the same.

That evening, Ray thought about what he had seen. In his head, he saw hundreds of McDonald's restaurants just like this one. All would have Multimixers!

He and the McDonald brothers signed a contract. Ray would start a chain of restaurants like the McDonald's in San Bernadino. He would use their name. They had already designed a new building with golden arches, and Ray would also use that design.

In 1955, Ray opened a McDonald's in Des Plaines, Illinois. From the beginning, the restaurant was busy.

Ray was busy too. Besides running the restaurant, he was still selling Multimixers. In spite of everything, Ray still found time to look for new locations to build more restaurants. He wanted his new business to grow.

Did it grow! After five years, Ray had opened 228 McDonald's restaurants. By then, Ray no longer wanted to be partners with the McDonald brothers. He paid them over two million dollars for their share of the company.

By 1972, Ray had 2,000 restaurants all across America. All told, the restaurants had sold over 10 billion hamburgers. Before long there were McDonald's restaurants throughout the world.

To teach employees how to run McDonald's restaurants, Ray opened Hamburger University. There new managers learned everything they needed to know. The school motto was "Quality, Service, Cleanliness, and Value." Those were the four things that made McDonald's restaurants successful.

Ray reached his goal of becoming rich. In fact, he became a millionaire. He spent some of his money on things he wanted, such as a mansion, a ranch, and a private jet. He even bought a baseball team, The San Diego Padres.

Much of his money, though, has been given away to help other people. He has helped hospitals, scientists, museums, and libraries. Ronald McDonald houses have been built next to many hospitals. There families can stay for almost free to be near their sick children.

Can you imagine the world without McDonald's? Ray Kroc was always a dreamer. He died in 1984, but his dream lives on.

Reaching Your Goal

What are your goals? Here are some steps to help you reach them.

1. **Decide on your goal.**
   It may be a short-term goal like one of these:
   learning to ride a bike
   getting a good grade on a test
   keeping your room clean
   It may be a long-term goal like one of these:
   learning to read
   learning to play the piano
   becoming a lawyer

2. **Decide if your goal is something you really can do.**
   Do you have the talent you need?
   How can you find out? By trying!
   Will you need special equipment?
   Perhaps you need a piano or ice skates.
   How can you get what you need?
   Ask your teacher or your parents.

3. Decide on the first thing you must do.
Perhaps this will be to take lessons.

4. Decide on the second thing you must do.
Perhaps this will be to practice every day.

5. Start right away.
Stick to your plan until you reach your goal.

6. Keep telling yourself, "I can do it!"

Good Luck! Maybe some day you will become a millionaire like Ray Kroc!

Reaching Your Goal Books

Beverly Cleary She Makes Reading Fun

Bill Cosby Superstar

Jesse Jackson A Rainbow Leader

Ted Kennedy, Jr. A Lifetime of Challenges

Christa McAuliffe Reaching for the Stars

Dale Murphy Baseball's Gentle Giant

Dr. Seuss We Love You

Samantha Smith Young Ambassador

Michael Jordan A Team Player

Steven Spielberg He Makes Great Movies

Charles Schulz Great Cartoonist

Cher Movie Star

Ray Kroc Famous Restaurant Owner

Hans Christian Andersen A Fairy Tale Life

Henry Cisneros A Hard Working Mayor

Jim Henson Creator of the Muppets

Rourke Enterprises, Inc.
P.O. Box 3328
Vero Beach, FL 32964

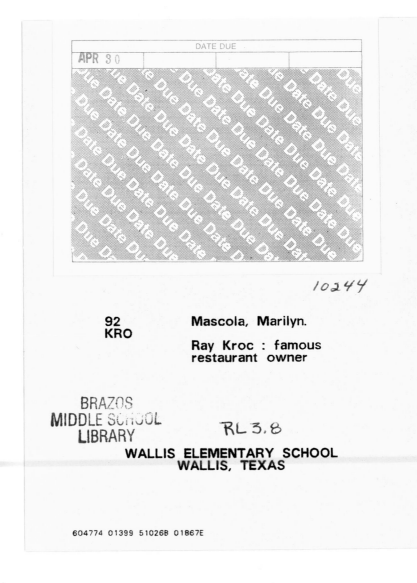